AF342167

The Hierarchies of Rue

BOOKS BY ROGER SAULS

Hard Weather
The Hierarchies of Rue

The Hierarchies of Rue

poems by Roger Sauls

Carnegie Mellon University Press
Pittsburgh 2000

ACKNOWLEDGMENTS

Grateful acknowledgment is made to the editors of the
following publications in which some of these poems
first appeared:

The Asheville Poetry Review, Shenandoah, and the
anthology *Buck and Wing: Southern Poetry at 2000.*

Publication of this book is supported by a grant from the
Pennsylvania Council on the Arts.

Library of Congress Catalog Card Number 98-71948
ISBN 0-88748-289-9 Pbk.

Printed and bound in the United States of America

10 9 8 7 6 5 4 3 2 1

CONTENTS

3.

1 PHENOMENOLOGY

November, 1993

The first cold snap. A pine vole breaks
into a run in front of me
on the walk, disappearing into itself,
the first of the season's extinctions.
Everywhere in the yard are pieces
of limbs, crooked oak
and broken poplar. I pick them up
for firewood and study the prose
in their bark. Love, it says,
is an intuition requiring clear days.
But this afternoon everything's blurred,
even sound has no edge,
and I have this cold
but avid need for the austere.
In a plain landscape
I look for the one detail
that defines what's missing,
the point where definitions vanish
and I think I'm on the verge
of some new kind of discourse.
A pond's surface blue with ice
can start it. It can make me
stop and talk to myself
about defects, while the weather
mills the horizon into fractals.
Like breath, I make conversation
without even knowing it,
the same way the steaming
dray horse licks a speech
deep into its own rough block of salt.
Yes, love is the one speech
I want to recite now, while the world

suddenly is a new idiom,
an idea I can run my hand along
over and over, never
making it threadbare.

Instructions on Confronting an Aromatic Plant

Break off a leaf and smell it—
it could be camphor, chamomile,
perhaps one of the consoling orders of poplar.
Crumble it between the thumb
and forefinger, roll it thoughtfully
as if it were part of your mind.
Be reminded, thus, that the inner life
is pungent, that like a leaf
it is its own galaxy. Look, the moon
in its tree is a kind of leaf, too,
one that the mind can't lift
from its place in the heavens,
that no fulcrum can move
from the poise of its perfect rest.

Weightlessness

1.
Even after I could name
a small bird like the curlew
and spot its twitch

in a field of dry grass,
I didn't know
how much wind it would take

to lift its spirit.

2.
It was a sight,
me hugging a corner
of the sedge,

the curlew steady,
the two of us a salt
mixed in the wind.

The scratch and speed
of things in a hurry,
the acumen of rush.

The body always
subject to blur.

3.
I lay for a time
in the dirt,
a hymn

in the wind's slur
of musical notes.
In a field like this

there's room only
for more dead.
Terrain is what lies

at the bottom of a life.

Hollow Creek Sequence

1.
In the country we talk about
the quality of dirt,

about crops, strategies
for planting.

And some of us just stand by the road looking,
nothing to do,

wondering about the grave, how far
it is to the vanishing point.

2.
In May I began to study the oak.
I watched the reaching and forking of its twigs,
the leafing out of its seasonal minutiae.

In October I split it with an axe,
looked at it in cross-section.

I understood how the years
had made it great.

3.
The fields here are fallow now,
girt and snaked by ancient walls.
I think about the masons whose hands weighed
so many stones, picking them out, lifting
and choosing them until tremors
in the wrists must have told them
the right weight.

Hollow Creek Sequence

4.
November. I praise the season
by noting its slow
slide into color, then pity

the friable ghosts it makes
of leaves as they slip
the noose of belonging.

5.
Fall, winter.
Two points along a plane.

Remember the mathematics
of the hinge and the shaft. Some night
you'll need a way out, a means

to escape from snow, or rain,
or from your own introspection.
Doors should work. Escape should be possible.

And the fuel oil, the propane.
Remember to store up your guile.
Let everything go.

6.
In spring, listen.
Even the slow traveling rake
of the harvester makes its own analysis
as it moves over the hayfields—

the empty sound of completion.

Work so clean
has to stop only for darkness.

7.
Meek sun smearing open the sky.

Stay here, you'll have to drop
seed to mark your place in time.

Insomnia

1.
Four a.m. By now the body has given up
its hope for the wage of sleep
it thinks it's owed. Actually, I'm penniless,
lying alone, reading this book,
William James's *A Pluralistic Universe.*
The world, it says, is a star
of flux and season,
an epic of blur, the sky itself
leaflike, threatening to fly off
from the tree it's earned.

2.   Eight A.M.
Outside, fog hangs thick
on the elms. The near distance is gone.
James says a spirit is attached
to the visible, but not so much
that it can be seen.
In the same way, hills take on
a shimmer after certain occurrences
of frost. If morning is the finest distinction
the day makes, I'll just wait
here for instruction.

3.
You know how a partridge sounds?
The watery, worried note
that follows the jerk sideways
of its shapely head?
Then it moves through tall grass
toward some dream it knows.
The body is always preparing itself for joy.

Late Autumn

These elm trees
in wind exist
as a text, their scribble
a description
of a world in ecstatic decline.

*

The eye, of course,
cannot discern
motion. The mind
instead knocks over
structure; the light
then shines up
through the ruin.

*

What's left
is a remnant of sky,
the season itself
faded and thin—
a scrap waiting
for strokes from a brush.

*

The secret of calligraphy
is swiftness and grace,
no stroke thicker
than a winter day.

*

The elm, bare now.

Like monks
they shed their public faces
to look inward.

*

What is prayer
but quick marks against darkness,
a tree or a mind,
a kind of dance
occuring just outside thought?

At the Beginning of September

Almost a week of rain.
The creek rushing
with hazards.

Joy now becomes
indistinguishable
from sadness—

life's moments
of grief are deployed

in time
as a kind of faith.
What's left

is to give thanks
for the month's
name, *September,*

September, brittle
as the sound
of cracking wood.

He Works Out His Solitude

1.
Dropping the pail, he waits.
If there's pitch and woof

in depth, hear
the moment as a sound,

the lyric of hitting bottom.

2.
Winter, the well glazed and hard.
He goes out in March

with his axe and works. Look at the way
they fly, the pieces each

beautiful according to their flaws.

3.
Then he tends the apples, their blooms
a home truth.

He makes order, his mind
avidly leafing

in the sadder perceptions.

4.
He rests. He thinks description
is a pencil mark

that approximates appearance.
When he needs a picture

he goes to specifics, rests in them. Sleeps.

5.
At dusk he knows the sounds.
Still he goes to the well,

draws up a voluble load.
He worries about the stars

while there's enough light.

6.
What dark does to accident
it does also to his thought. Approaching solitude

as work he sees it
in the sense of getting to zero,

taking more and more drinks of himself.

It's Simple

Recognizing that in work
no redemption is earned
by the body's pain,

the Shakers devised long
handles for brooms.
A form of grace

to keep the back
straight—
they meant

a broom to help move
the self up
toward the joyous.

Then they could sweep,
all day dignified,
make the world

clean for once, and plain.

Waking

I couldn't see the nuthatch
or the wren as they raked alphabets
on the dull tin of the gutter.
This early, waking is a kind of weather,
a fog, perhaps, that you meet
on the way to the mind's next landscape.
So I set out for the yard, where grackles
threw pebbles in the air for joy.

Months Off

Down here, napping on the earth.
I gaze up at the sky

and the clouds that look like plowed fields.
Harvest is months off, though.

There's only the heat and the simmer
of late afternoon's deep look

into itself.
When the wind finally rises, high

and blue, my head starts to clear,
the release like a spring

slowly paying out all its fine tension.

History

As in the surface of an ancient Chinese vase,
flaws have already appeared in its glaze.
We know we can strip away most
of its failure, but there's still damage,
and we understand so little of the oblique.

First Instruction in Prayer

Once, when departing birds
rose from the elms in thrashing vowels,

I learned to make my own speech
a perfection of o's. At night

on my knees I'd repeat words from the big
black book I had, its pages

rippling with joyous sentences.
O my God, I'd say.

I could feel the heart
inside me turning. I remembered

the way my bicycle felt
under me when we glided,

how sometimes I fused
with the continuous downpour

of its blue metal.
With so much motion

in me it was impossible
not to believe. O, I could see myself

being carried off by angels
and dropped in the sky like a twig to grow.

The Notion that Sleep Amends

Lying there late in bed the idea
made me content—
to let my dream's great snow

cover and change me, then spill
into the dark the small hills
my body made under the quilts.

Created over that way just once,
how could I want anything
again from the known world?

Even the perfectly-blue dusks
of late February could not
stir me. I wanted only to relax

once more under a snow thrown down
from a great height. And when
the time came I thought the change

would move into me privately,
and shining I'd awake in some
new place, where perhaps

choirs had just left,
their hymnals still open,
fluttering on the pews.

Sleep

I bend my back, touch one hand
to my forehead. That way
when the dream arrives, it won't
pass straight through.

It Comes Apart in the Hand

If dusk was not enough to console me,
now there's snow, its random slurs
sticking briefly to the window. That quickly

a grief can pass, its perishableness
one of the afternoon's details
that falter routinely into dream.

After all, doesn't the whole day
blink shut into nothing but a smear
of blue refractions? And that gray bird

whose lament lasts past supper,
isn't its song about the diminishment
of us all into nothing?

Stepping into the dark I hesitate,
afraid I might take a wrong turn.
I just want my soul to roll out

once and shine like a moon, that porous stone
that comes apart in the hand.
I won't sleep tonight. I'll press my face to the glass

like the child who once heard
the stillness of ice healing
and now waits for the skaters to pass.

4 A.M.

Out on the porch, it was still dark.
The April sky had been teased out

in places like loose threads.
Nearby, the moon shone like a knifeblade.

It would be the perfect crime, I thought,
to force stillness like this on the world,

to make even the harping sparrows observe
a new polity of silence.

Up the street the lights of the first cars
were picking up

the neighborhood's landmarks,
polishing the streets into glass.

I just stood there. I'd seen it before—
Cold flakes would soon ignite

in deep places in the wind,
and rows of houses would turn to leaves.

Anyway, what was there to hear?
The muttering of the hills?

The bare trees perfecting their stillness?
I moved from side to side,

pretending to kick at pieces of kindling.
The stars were little matchflares

and I still had plenty of time
to be righteous about the grace of my failures.

Play Than I

No sooner have I learned my part in the play
than I see this matchbox
and wonder why it isn't in the play, too.

Stopping for Coffee in South Carolina

1.
A little east of Ideal, the road curves.
I slip out of my body a minute, the road
still jumping at the back of my eyes.

A light comes on in the diner, then another.
I watch as little articles of me rise
through the fluorescence, tiny bicycles
headed for the moon, pedals lazily turning.

I say, Flight is an understanding
some creatures have with death,
that grace is always worth the risk.

2.
The most significant journeys commence
at dusk, in the rain. The drive home
is what I'm dreading now, the blurred

and smeared sun just visible beyond
the window, the cup of coffee in my hand
a dead star. And these pink,
pearl, and gray thunderheads

promise a revelation. This could be
the kind of rain that lashes
and hurts, the kind that breaks bones.

At Faulkner's Rowan Oak

I promised myself once I'd honor the great
by forgiving them their private
and unbearable pasts, and by letting them
lie still for all time. Even so,
in Oxford for a day, I couldn't resist
driving up to Old Taylor Road, and finding
his house, that minor work they say he loved.

I wanted no harm to come from my interest,
so I stood a moment outside the fence.
I could feel the hot August wind move me
solicitously toward the front walk, and I set
foot on the same brick herringbone
that he had, and tottered a little under the weight.

At the closed front door, no one in sight,
I wondered if I was supposed to knock.
I wanted some kind of forgiveness in advance,
his permission, perhaps, to open the door.
But I went in anyway, wary, telling myself
that even if he were here, he probably would not
look up at my approach, or be distracted
by the noise I'd let in, or by anything
bearing the dust of the recently fallen world.

William Faulkner's Khaki Pants at Rowan Oak

Frayed at the cuffs, out in the knees.
Thrown with exquisite carelessness
across the bed by some curator.

It looks as though he left them there
in the night, returned from consulting
his failures, drunk on the best bourbon.

In the end, though, I knew it had been a case
of utter exhaustion.

Some Analogue

Think of the blackberry bog as an assertion
of our condition. Or its corollary,

the mud in a deer's hoof. As if *earth*
referred to some analogue of the self,

some place that's a world
of older design. Everything we are exists

between the false and the imperfectly known.
Think of the way our bones fly

out of our bodies and into the stars.

Footnote to a Certain Novel

You must've noticed, it feels cold
when time closes on you.
A mystery rises from the stillness
of what's left, breath,
and there's the onset of fear. You remember
how morning air stalls
a moment, and the sky is lucid blue.
You're close to death then,
as if it were a thing you found in the shadows,
some kind of knowledge,
or a craft you could take up and perfect.

Two Inquiries about Salvation

1.
Augustine said it, the divines
did not talk to each other, only
to time, so I went with myself

into the cornfields, and sang
that I might be delivered, me,
a man enclosed by refusals, with no true

beginning, like night, and I sang
that someone receive me, not just for now, but for always,
for my sins were sufficiently great.

2.
There is a certain blue, I've noticed it
in May, at night, and I can't sleep
some nights because of it, and no,

the concessions I make to God do not ease
the weight of it, or how
it wears me, touching me and parting

like regret, this blue, a certain blue
I know by heart, it's in me,
I've noticed it, in May, at night.

The Trappist Monastery in Conyers

Set back in the trees

the mock Gothic sanctuary
was stained by shadows and light.
Around it, low hills lapsed across
the fields as if to show how pride
could be edified into grace.
As we approached, walking down a path
where tulip poplars spilled cool basilicas
of shade at our feet, we stopped
to admire the arduous work
God had put into the moment. A plane
was overhead, the size of an insect,
and between us a poise
as perfect as the mercies of the infinite.

Solitude

This is what I want, I said. Joy.
The joy of a man
from whose shoe a stone has just been shaken.

The Hierarchies of Rue

1.
Like art, apples invite small licks
of color to their making,
pigments of orange and yellow, chips of blue,
brown, and green, hues
in every variation, the many shades of a theme—

i.e., that a thing containing itself, for instance,
contains you.

Protein, sodium, potassium. An Esopus Spitzenburg
of five ounces is simple enough
in that way to describe.

Here in the hand, though, hard as a planet,
it's more complex. When cradled and held—
a watercolor, a landscape full of tint.

Eat it, it's something else.
With apples, you get to the core
directly.

You feel sorrow, regret, grief,
all the hierarchies of rue.

And living it,
begin to contain yourself
in a crisp peel of contrition.

2.
As children we climbed the stunted
trees and shook

until the lyric fall
of apples filled

our glee—
the ultimate joy

to bring all the nubbins down.
A wheeling rain of leaves, too,

from the top limbs, yellow
and transparent as melancholy.

On the ground we say
the apple carries the only

phenomenology that matters.

3.
All October the articulate
blue of rain. I resolve

again to reconcile
the ways of apples,

to hold them accountable
to their myths.

About survival,
what do their rough skins

have to teach me,
about doubt is their patient sleep

inside the syrups
of xylum an example,

can their liquor heal the damage
done by long silence on the ground?

I longed to understand
the cidery doubt

in the Braeburn's heart,
in the Cortland's aromatic flesh.

Harmony, I thought, is the heft
in the curve of the Twenty Ounce,

the love the hand has
for the Freyberg's sweeping back.

4.
Is it true, though, that the apple exists
only to excite the hand?

I think about it as I trudge into the orchard,
into the rain burdened
afternoon with Wellies and slicker
to scavenge what's fallen
and lost.

Look, so many Haralsons crumbling here,
so many withered Baldwins.

Is it true? I know the apple exists
to permit inventories of contrition—
Arlets, Knobbed Russets, the misshapen
toll of regret the spirit feels
on rainy days.

One of the promises of redemption, surely,
is that the body may subside
into darkness, but matter's great
need is to become soil again,
to permit flowering and fragrance.

Hold that Criterion up to the light,
fondle it the way a penitent touches
his remorse. The blossoms bob
and dawdle on the spindly limbs, speaking
of rue, how it's an art
colored by time and too much thought.

2 MERCY

Snowfall in New Jersey

It happened that snow rose up in the east
and all night it prospered.
By noon your yard was a glory
of fattened barns and shelters,
the wealth of the whole farm
a matter of sums and joinery—

Later I followed you out the door,
both of us carrying large-handled shovels.
As we dug from the yard's
opposite ends, we met in the middle.
That was our wisdom, for we had decided
that to meet halfway was a good beginning,
to simply start down the crooked path
of human endeavor. So we leaned there
on our shovels. In a storm
of revelations we'd begun to know each other.

We were tired but could feel
a kind of joy growing in us, a joy
specific to winter, in fact to this snow,
and we knew its only explanation
was that it had fallen.

Late

Late November. The weather
could go either way.

We'd come to the end, though,
argument and storm

the only thing between us.
When it was quiet,

our words stilled
in cold setting in,

how we felt fear
leap in us like flushed doves.

The quick bicker of wings,
the gradual settling of dark.

We stood near the house,
led finally out of language,

all our tricks gone,
and we could see light

in the kitchen, even hear
the gas ring hiss

in the still
place beneath the kettle.

Her

What is it a man hones
smooth by a few odd uses,

nicks and hacks
by his hurt, keeps

worn down by care
or error, what does he turn

like a mood,
side to back, slow

as the plod of a mare?
It's her and the way

she's close, as ease
is close to vetch

running in the dirt
all over him.

St. Matthew's Cemetery, Hillsborough, NC

We had gone to one of those fields in the country
where headstones were the only reliable crop.
It was winter, January damp as wings.
That year she had become infatuated
with a certain kind of art, one where form
involved complex departures from itself,
as here, where she could see how wind
had made notable consultations
with good stone. Occasionally it rained,
or snowed, and sometimes you could hear
the dead practicing Latin, their phrasing
grand and round, repeating the names
of stars and their cognates,
now the dead's only family. Occasionally
she'd try to brush time
from the marble, put her face close
to its cryptic clues. But mostly she took notes,
alert as a crow, writing out everything,
everything, this long confession from God.

The Owl is an Elegy

So we listen as Neal, our carpenter, tells us one day
about his deaths. That's how he describes them—
how he lapses into calm when the sound of an owl
breaks open the quiet. Everything inside him
stops then, he says. And it happens on a roof,
for instance, while he snaps the dusty chalk string
that makes the ghostly trail he'll line up the shingles by.
He'll swoon a moment then in midair and pray
that all the while the earth is at the same height
as the substance of his mind. It's the way he's come
to talk to us now, amiably blurting out his fears,
the startling sins and joys of his life. One day
he looks at us and says he needs a nail, he just doesn't know
what size, and begins to fish in his box
for the right tool. That's when he laughs.
He says there was another time, it happened
in the yard after late supper while he talked
with his daughter. He felt water moving
in his bones, his spine a minor creek. He's old, he says,
and by now knows the self must be small,
perhaps the size of a ruffled, soft bird,
one whose song is said to ascend to prophecy.
He knows, too, that talk does not grant him
exemption from the silence of that other life,
but work will lift him, as always, to the arts beyond
the knowledge of his own shaking hands.

Work

She works all morning
with a rake. Later rests

beside me and describes jewel weed,
how easily it sways

in the May wind, as if
such ease meant it had found peace.

She knows, too, about the motionless—
how even a steady mind eventually dissolves

like rain's faint empire
when it begins to let its borders fall.

May's over now.
She needs stones,

small ones for paths,
large ones for boundaries.

It Filled Me

Last night rain
fell in vectors and you
found geometry
in the way an orange
fell apart in sections,
its secrets opened up.
Strange comfort to think
a life can be composed
entirely of lines.
I just wanted to sharpen
a handful of pencils and draw
us a life the size
of an oak, its root
system larger than this house.

Young Deer

Dusk is the permission the shy ones
need to come out,
the awkward, odd ones

with sidelong grace,
the browsers in chicory
who will never learn to dance.

There is a kind of lover
with these same traits,
the indirect ones

who have no courage except
in shadows, as here
where dusk stalls color

in its race through
the outer world, slowing
thought, darkening passion.

Pleasure

The way the moon slides
through its phases, waning

its own halos away.
The word moon eliding

its own consonants,
leaving behind new moons.

Think about it—
the word moon makes moons

by erosion, leaving just
two vowels, new moons.

I mean, think about
the moon. Think about pleasure.

The Morning After

I woke in the morning dirt,
my head still shaking. I must have resembled

a dog unpuzzling itself
from sleep, convulsively renewed.

Not that I understood why, or could explain
the reason my knowledge refused

to give its terms directly.
But there they were in the trees,

the ribbons and blouses
that proved the existence of angels.

At the Anasazi Ruins in Northern Arizona

For a long time we gazed solemnly
across that wide canyon, trying to discern

in the distance the round windows
and entrances in the cliffs, the jutting

dusty rooflines of the tiny apartments.
What kind of art their lives

must have required, where the simplest act,
taking place on a precipice,

demanded grace and nerve.
That afternoon we could see

it was almost a mile down
and only the crows casually riding thermals

seemed not to sense the danger.
We were there for the silence,

hoping that to isolate our love
in that ancient place would help us

understand how to make love continue.
No one knows why but

one day the Anasazi were gone—
they had no genius for the future.

In one way I want us always
to be like them, living a pure form

of daring, risking it all every day
in order to live courageously in the present.

Supper

On the windowsill
you have arranged green peppers
whose waxy skins hold the smell of this morning's rain.

Later you will take them up
with perfect compassion and begin to slice.

That way you will show me love, how the point
is always the care you bring to the object.

Pole Beans

Between us we hold the string taut.
I wait while the shoots
work out the details of thrust

and braid. When it begins to happen,
you make a sound.
A crosshatch finally appears,

tendrils curled
and forked by the hundreds.
It's you.

I say we have to keep working
at this. Our bodies shake
in the wet blue of the dark.

Summer: A Complaint

A late swim, then we drank neat rum
and watched dusk turn the river
the color of figs. Our bodies

stayed wet for a long time, and once
we stood suddenly still, thinking we heard
voices of people we couldn't see.

We liked that fear, the idea that
respect for death is essential
to proper happiness. We didn't think

then of time or anything
extending beyond the filmy ease
of our mutual need. And though touch

was everything that moment,
we found it entirely agreeable
not to know what came next.

If music is the underside of hearing,
this breeze is the talk we'll sing
about later, one day when

it's over and we'll recall this surrender,
how it became so dense
it was a kind of vegetation.

Like An Apple

I promised myself I'd touch her
like an apple. But what I touched

was sadness, its roundness also
like an apple, its slope falling

away into melancholy, voluptuous,
its curves impossible to hold in the head.

The Myth of Rainbows

I thought of the Ark, the sorrow
of rain as it lifted the saved
at the same time death's volume rose.

And the bird on the horizon,
its one mistake was to think

navigation is only sensing an edge.
I made it to shore, in galas of high wind.
The sin was all on my side.

Loss: An Introduction

1.
The part he couldn't get over was the weight,
the authentic crack of each bone
in his spine when the sadness was laid on.
That was later.

Now it was a summer night.
He'd come home late
and learned she'd left.

After the first faint thrill
of fear he'd felt when he learned it,
there was the general onset of terror, the loss,
so many hard
days and nights he knew
he'd have to get through.

As the truth set in,
he recognized the manifest
evidence of his failure,
the crush of dead weight
he couldn't withstand—

over, a few months worth of marriage.

2.
July was when it started,
illusions falling
in the high summer humidity.

She was this, he was that.
None of it fit.

And the weeks and weeks
of dark rain and chill had done such harm.

So many gray days, so much loss.

He could still hear her weeping,
the deep tremor in the verbs
when she spoke.

He drove south, home,
alone in his roaming car.
Back in a week, late,

he wanted her in the dark.
But there was nothing,
the house empty

of her slips and skirts, gone
the immense literature
of her presence in the rooms.

Instead there was a black
terrified bird loose
in his mind.

3.
The idea of right exists, he'd thought.
It was from that place
he'd argued his heart.

She'd argued. They'd argued.

Now he wanted her,
her angles and bones
on his skin with its pain.

4.
How to extract from loss
some brave new grace
and reason to live.

He had hoped for love
so unassailable the spirit of it
would have the hard force

of a storm. Instead, he was cracked
at the bone by a gale.
He was cut by flying glass.

Now he just wanted
to slip past her
as if she were liquid.

5.
How often a life
is kindled, one stick at a time,
only to be used

to light a fire.
His anger, that was the storm
she said was between them.

Not so, to him. Rather the conviction
that some wrong thing inside
him would never be righted,

and he could never make her understand.

After You Left

1.
After you left, I began to study
the literature of solitude.
The Cloud of Unknowing, Thoreau
keeping a journal, drunk
at his lonely pond.

For weeks I hid in the orchard,
a scholar of loss
among the rough Spys and Jonathans.

2.
Every day I'd be up
with the whistling of black tree sparrows,
coffee or tea with berries
for breakfast.

All morning clouds were wild with high wind.

And I'd say *A man must know
the sweep and roll of his sadness,
the full swell of his direst thought.*

3.
It came down finally to breakage.
I knew from myth
that at the end of discord
a new harmony may often be born.

But all I could do at the end was count
my bones and walk off
that bleak and starry hill,
the cicadas in the dirt
saying your name, *broken, broken.*

4.
Listen—after that I could hear
the Jonathans begin to fall.
the Spys loud in the grass with lamentation.

By then I compared everything
to an apple, anyway.

5.
As when color
begins to cover an apple,
one hemisphere
of agreement meeting another,

reconciliation, when it happens,
moves out cumulatively
from a center, as an apple's
curt pain does when it ripens.

3

Bringing Water to the Dead

This is the earth
he drove his harrows over,
their blades turning up
the inner life of the soil,

the peace of its water.
This was his city,
the toil beneath the loam,
histories of drought

and plenty. This was his farm.

The century mostly gone,
his days cracked by hard labor. And when the hills

in his mind dimmed,
back canted to one side,
he'd go out anyway, body rocking
for hours on the tractor seat.

Rain's arrival, its specifics, its drift
and fall into his thinking
haunted him. It made the crops,
he prayed. Mercy to the lonely

seeds in the field,
he repeated. Have mercy.
And to the flare
of summer lightning he ordered

Let there be rain. Oh, he hoped.
Inside, frowned. His brow would scroll
with worry and crack

like old wood. The day's heat

disbanding and separating,
the tin rattle
of irrigation, the soy bean fields
trembling beneath it,
the sky full
of the rocketry of water.

Postscript

It was March, still too early to give up
the melancholy of late winter. The north
pasture still brown and sopping,
and beyond it skinny hardwoods that shimmered
the cursive prose of final chapters.

Grandfather, you were there too. I remember
you beside the porch rail, holding on
to your last year. We talked some about death,
your face pained but chiseled to dignity
by the faint seasonal light.

Absorbed by the many ghostly forms of dusk,
you looked out at the quickly dimming world.
It was almost freezing. The chill made your breath
visible, a spirit you conjured up out of nothing.
You stood there quietly, though your head must have hummed

like an unruly school of rocking chairs.
I thought of the stories you told in your graying
voice, the stories from your hard youth—
the early mornings you'd go collect kindling,
nested it carefully in the hearth.

From a deep pocket you'd retrieve an Ohio Blue Tip,
drag it thoughtfully over the hearth's
rough brick, making the whole conjugation
flare. Tonight it's you burning in the dusk, in places
no one can name. Watching you add this postscript

to the history of your breath, I knew you were becoming
part of the air. And when you went inside later
to stand near the fire, I stayed outside
and listened as a light rain began to recite
all the known definitions of *shine*.

My Grandfather Photographed With a Mandolin, 1916

He stood dignified in a blue suit
too loose for a man so small, frowning
against the torrents of light
thrown down in August in south Georgia.
The dirt around him was full
of sweet watermelon scent, and he had begun
to understand the spell cast by women.
He held his head still, to one side,
as everything in hearing waited
for its moment to dance. It was simple—
when the time came she would arrive
and he would shoulder his instrument
decisively, drive his mind
deep into the curvature
of that ample music, its arcs
flowing through him like whiskey.

Hubert By Name

At first light we'd go

into the elements to find birds,
or sit with the cattails,

drink their dank friendliness and sway.
Hours of this, years.

A moment came, though,

and he left. I remember his grace
when he departed, the strange elegance

of his limbs as he flew.

Anthony Michael Sauls
b. 4/13/90 d. 7/01/90

When the first rush
of pulse stirred
in your startled flesh

I think I heard it.
A bright noise
that scared me from sleep.

I still hear it
in the dark's mutter,
and wonder what you knew

that first night, suddenly
alive, but so small
in the tumult of the planet

you were barely a flicker.
And though your skin
when I finally touched it

was bridged and laddered
with bruise-colored veins,
I saw only one

or two short roads
going out toward daylight.
Beside you the landscape

of your life
was a tiny country,
your name its only inhabitant.

I Was Twelve

The idea I had was to rise early,
to slip into the morning before
its thrashing could distract me.

No light yet, and I'd made it
above the tree line. I was twelve.
That was before I knew the name

for solitude, but I liked the words
left on my glasses by snow.
Words like *enigma*. And *fugue*.

It all went through me, invisible.
I'd fuse with it with the ease
of light entering a kitchen window.

By the stove my mother worried
the day's first fire into life, stirring
this and that with most of her mind.

Where is he, she was always wondering.
Some day he'll go up
as suddenly as a kitchen match.

When I Killed the Snake with a Hoe

I understood at some point that I'd finished,
and felt the flat feel
of death tingling at the end
of my fingers. Only ten,

I already knew the best things
shimmered with fear.
I could sense them taking shape
around me, their edges

both present and disappearing.
The perfectly black
menace of the broken snake
whirled and glittered

at my feet like collapsed electricity.
How it had squirmed, turning
and twisting, surprised by my bright
striking metal.

In my hand I saw the hoe.
I felt my hot mind
begin to drift back into my head.
I knew that life passed in pieces

and I couldn't say
if it was good or bad.
I just knew
I couldn't wait till this was over.

The Hay

The only thing to do now was listen
to the chatter of bridles swaying,
the exhalations of many tired horses.

The pain. Impossible at this hour not to think
of the body as a broken tree.

The hope is that night will arrive soon
in its ancient blue conveyance, welcome
but so slow it will save no one.

It's the time of hay, the time of bent backs
infinite across the purpling hills.

Anthony Michael Sauls
b. 4/13/90   d. 7/01/90

In my arms you were flawlessly still,
looking back while I studied the grave
expression my chromosomes had given you,
a few shadows making speculations on your brow.
When you died I thought my grief
must have no bottom. It was exquisite,
like your own perfect abandonment to calm.
Now I think how much I still need
to talk to you, missing you. My own life
so serious and sad, like a great rain
in the night that touches down everywhere at once.

At the Cemetery
for M.

Now the lights go dead in the blue
thin air of May. The sticks fall
in a rain from the elms,

and we put aside everyday talk.
If the day has gone, we say
let it. We do solemnly grieve

its going, but the legacy of grace
is that stars come out
only in the dark. Some day

the star of our own grief
also will blow away, taking with it
the flaws in our affection. In the stillness here

there's a car or two, a low fence, black trees—
each is an object with its own hum.
Waiting quietly, we understand there's a limit

on the weight things can bear, they told us so,
but nobody mentioned how intricate
your departure would be, its soil so much lighter than air.

Dreaming of My Mother's Death

In the kudzu and trumpet vine,
I was not afraid. I was drenched
the same as if a storm had passed.

I watched her body travel through zones
of different music, and moor
in silence on the other side.

The one thing I knew
had become speakable at last.
 I could say out loud that I loved her.

It was the truth, with penumbras.
In the sweet agricultural smells
of Georgia, crickets made their own shiny songs.

Some Child

I was thinking back, and the blue twists
of falling rain helped spice

the old memories. What spilled out of the dark
was my mother, forlorn on the front stoop

calling me to come back and get a coat.
For all I knew she was talking to some child

she'd heard about in a song, not me.
In fact, her words were only a hum, a lullaby

perhaps meant for herself. Calling out to me
was the last form her loneliness took.

I ignored her.
Because the dying spin so rapidly into the next world,

they can't hear. The wind was blowing her away
and I kept riding that gyroscope

in the air that turned and turned, holding on
to it, one arm stuck out to slice the rain.

Elementary Poem

When the rain comes, it brings a voice.
It's the voice of a father, a mild father
who says one thing over and over. *Here
I give you this dust to build a life with.*

Motionless

Some nights pieces of my grandfather's death
snake free from my dreams
and get loose in my life.
It happens in the hot summer—
wakened by any stark
sound from the street
I think it's him, his addled
calls that used to fly
down the stairwell as if he were a bird
being shooed away. Usually though,
he'd lie still on the bed, thin
blue fingers gripping the sheets,
time nosing coldly into him.
his body motionless
as water in a stone bowl.

Again and again these torrid nights,
I go looking for him
in my rooms, as tonight,
alert with fear I go to the windows,
the outdoors immense
with simple decoration, and see
stars coming out like mild
assertions of an authority
no one respects anymore.

Late Spring, South Georgia

After supper, while the family sat dead
tired in the heat of the parlor, some kind of fear
would whir in and circle us. Somebody would get up
casually and go shut the door.
Who was there? Outside, a lawn sprinkler would throw
messy stars into the dark. Was this the way
the earth sent up its own elegies?
At dusk we thought we heard them,
and we shuddered. We all knew the old things
needed rest. My grandfather would push back
his chair, fumble for words. It was only the predictable
grievances of the season, first one and then another
slipping into the dark, the warm dark
where everything flowered, became a star.

An Explanation of September

I have a click in my knee
when I bend, and the lisping
little places in my bones

make walking a strain,
my steps an odd
but luminous dance.

I see how the body
needs ways to find the grace
implied by its own decline.

Thus I look out,
knowing the day's ordinary mysteries
will fade, and choirs of its noise

will gather and part, the weather
leaving spare captions on the ground.
How easy to admit then

that death is the one
inducement to truth we acknowledge
without question, and thank God

for those times when it's best
just to sit watching
and some things will shine

the moment you think
the light in them
has started to die.

Draft of the Final Poem About My Grandfather

On killing days, blood spotted
my grandfather's shirt front.
He'd wring the necks of pullet

after pullet, never once letting
the cigarette in his lips die.
Back in the house

his talk was so mild
it quieted the room.
At times he'd look away

as if he'd heard
a thrush just leaving
its roost on the corncrib.

1995

Germany, Caroline Finkelstein
Housekeeping in a Dream, Laura Kasischke
About Distance, Gregory Djanikian
Wind of the White Dresses, Mekeel McBride
Above the Tree Line, Kathy Mangan
In the Country of Elegies, T. Alan Broughton
Scenes from the Light Years, Anne C. Bromley
Quartet, Angela Ball
Rorschach Test, Franz Wright

1996

Back Roads, Patricia Henley
Dyer's Thistle, Peter Balakian
Beckon, Gillian Conoley
The Parable of Fire, James Reiss
Cold Pluto, Mary Ruefle
Orders of Affection, Arthur Smith
Colander, Michael McFee

1997

Growing Darkness, Growing Light, Jean Valentine
Selected Poems, 1965-1995, Michael Dennis Browne
Your Rightful Childhood: New and Selected Poems, Paula Rankin
Headlands: New and Selected Poems, Jay Meek
Soul Train, Allison Joseph
The Autobiography of a Jukebox, Cornelius Eady
The Patience of the Cloud Photographer, Elizabeth Holmes
Madly in Love, Aliki Barnstone
An Octave Above Thunder: New and Selected Poems, Carol Muske

1998

Yesterday Had a Man In It, Leslie Adrienne Miller
Definition of the Soul, John Skoyles
Dithyrambs, Richard Katrovas
Postal Routes, Elizabeth Kirschner
The Blue Salvages, Wayne Dodd

The Joy Addict, James Harms
Clemency and Other Poems, Colette Inez
Scattering the Ashes, Jeff Friedman
Sacred Conversations, Peter Cooley
Life Among the Trolls, Maura Stanton

1999
Justice, Caroline Finkelstein
Edge of House, Dzvinia Orlowsky
*A Thousand Friends of Rain:
        New and Selected Poems, 1976-1998*, Kim Stafford
The Devil's Child, Fleda Brown Jackson
World as Dictionary, Jesse Lee Kercheval
Vereda Tropical, Ricardo Pau-Llosa
The Museum of the Revolution, Angela Ball
Our Master Plan, Dara Wier

2000
Small Boat with Oars of Different Size, Thom Ward
Post Meridian, Mary Ruefle
The Hierarchies of Rue, Roger Sauls
Constant Longing, Dennis Sampson
Mortal Education, Joyce Peseroff
How Things Are, James Richardson
Years Later, Gregory Djanikian